Notes a
Number 16, February 16, 1850

Various

Alpha Editions

This edition published in 2022

ISBN: 9789356898028

Design and Setting By

Alpha Editions
www.alphaedis.com

Email - info@alphaedis.com

Contents

NOTES
DANIEL DE FOE AND HIS GHOST STORIES

I feel obliged by your intelligent correspondent "D.S." having ascertained that De Foe was the author of the *Tour through Great Britain*. Perhaps he may also be enabled to throw some light on a subject of much curiosity connected with De Foe, that appears to me well worth the inquiry.

Mrs. Bray, in her General Preface prefixed to the first volume of the reprint, in series, of her *Novels and Romances*, when giving an account of the circumstances on which she founded her very graphic and interesting romance of *Trelawny of Trelawne*, says—

> "In Gilbert's *History of Cornwall*, I saw a brief but striking account, written by a Doctor Ruddell, a clergyman of Launceston, respecting a ghost which (in the year 1665) he has seen and laid to rest, that in the first instance had haunted a poor lad, the son of a Mr. Bligh, in his way to school, in a place called the 'Higher Broom Field.' This grave relation showed, I thought, the credulity of the times in which the author of it lived; and so I determined to have doctor, boy, and ghost in my story. But whereas, in the worthy divine's account of the transaction, the ghost appears to come on earth for no purpose whatever (unless it be to frighten the poor boy), I resolved to give the spirit something to do in such *post-mortem* visitations, and that the object of them should be of import to the tale. Accordingly I made boy, doctor, and the woman (who is said after her death to have appeared to the lad) into characters, invented a story for them, and gave them adventures."

Mrs. Bray adds—

> "Soon after the publication of *Trelawny*, my much esteemed friend, the Rev. F.V.T. Arundell[1], informed me, that, whilst engaged in his antiquarian researches in Cornwall, he found among some old and original papers the manuscript account, in Dr. Ruddell's own hand-writing, of his encounter with the ghost in question. This he lent Gilbert, who inserted it in his *History of Cornwall*; and there I first saw it, as stated above. A few months ago,

I purchased some of the reprinted volumes of the *Works of Daniel De Foe*. Among these was the *Life of Mr. Duncan Campbell*, a fortune-teller. To my great surprise, I found inserted in the Appendix (after verses to Mr. Duncan Campbell), without either name of the author, reference, or introduction, under the heading, 'A remarkable Passage of an Apparition, 1665,' no other than Dr. Ruddell's account of meeting the ghost which had haunted the boy, so much the same as that I had read in Gilbert, that it scarcely seemed to differ from it in a word. The name of Mr. Bligh, the father of the boy, was, however, omitted; and Dr. Ruddell could only be known as the author of the account by the lad's father calling the narrator Mr. Ruddell, in their discourse about the youth. The account is so strangely inserted in the Appendix to the volume, without comment or reference, that, had I not previously known the circumstances above names by Mr. Arundell, I should have fancied it a fiction of De Foe himself, like the story of the ghost of Mrs. Veal, prefixed to *Drelincourt on Death.*

"Aware that Mr. Arundell had no idea that Ruddell's ghost story was to be found in any work previous to Gilbert's, I lost no time in communicating to that gentleman what I could not but deem a very curious discovery. He assured me there could be no mistake as to the genuineness of the ghost document he had found, as he had compared the manuscript with Ruddell's hand-writing in other papers, and saw it was one and the same. Soon after, Mr. Arundell favoured me with some further information on the subject, which I here give, as it adds still more to the interest of the story:—'Looking into Gilbert's *History of Cornwall*, in the parish of South Petherwin, there is said to be in the old mansion of Botathan five portraits of the Bligh family; one of them is the likeness of the boy, whose intimacy with the ghost of Dorothy Durant has been spoken of in his first volume, where she is erroneously called Dingley. If this be a fact, it is very interesting; for it is strange that both Mr. Ruddell, the narrator (whose manuscript I lent to Gilbert), and De Foe, should have called her Dingley. I have no doubt it was a fictitious name, for I never heard of it Launceston or the neighbourhood; whereas Durant is the name of an ancient Cornish family: and I remember a tall, respectable man of that name in Launceston, who died at a very advanced age;

> very probably a connexion of the Ghost Lady. He must have been born about 1730. Durant was probably too respectable a name to be published, and hence the fictitious one.' Mr. Arundell likewise says, 'In Launceston Church is a monument to Charles Bligh and Judith his wife, who died, one in 1716, and the other in 1717. He is said to have been sixty years old, and was probably the brother of Samuel, the hero of Dorothy Dingley. Sarah, the wife of the Rev. John Ruddell, died in 1667. Mr. Ruddell was Vicar of Aternon in 1684. He was the minister of Launceston in 1665, when he saw the ghost who haunted the boy.'"

Such is Mrs. Bray's account of these very curious circumstances. The ghost story inserted in Gilbert, as mentioned above, is altogether so much in the style of De Foe, that a doubt remains whether, after all, he may not have been the author of it. Can "D.S.," or any of your readers, throw further light on the subject?

D.S.Y.

Footnote 1: (return) Of Landulph, Cornwall, the author of *Discoveries in Asia Minor*, and the well-known *Visit to the Seven Churches of Asia*. Mr. Arundell is now dead.

PET-NAMES

"Mary" is informed that "Polly" is one of those "hypocorisms," or pet-names, in which our language abounds. Most are mere abbreviations, as Will, Nat, Pat, Bell, &c., taken usually from the beginning, sometimes from the end of the name. The ending *y* or *ie* is often added, as a more endearing form: as Annie, Willy, Amy, Charlie, &c. Many have letter-changes, most of which imitate the pronunciation of infants. *L* is lisped for *r.* A central consonant is doubled. *O* between *m* and *l* is more easily sounded than *a.* An infant forms *p* with its lips sooner than *m*; papa before mamma. The order of change is: Mary, Maly, Mally, Molly, Polly. Let me illustrate this; *l* for *r* appears in Sally, Dolly, Hal *P* for *m* in Patty, Peggy; vowel-change in Harry, Jim, Meg, Kitty, &c; and in several of these the double consonant. To pursue the subject: re-duplication is used; as in Nannie, Nell, Dandie; and (by substitution) in Bob. Ded would be of ill omen; therefore we have, for Edward, Ned or Ted, *n* and *t* being coheir to *d*; for Rick, Dick, perhaps on account of the final *d* in Richard. Letters are dropped for softness: as Fanny for Franny, Bab for Barb, Wat for Walt. Maud is Norman for Mald, from Mathild, as Bauduin for Baldwin. Argidius becomes Giles, our nursery friend Gill, who accompanied Jack in his disastrous expedition "up the hill." Elizabeth gives birth to Elspeth, Eliza (Eloisa?), Lisa, Lizzie, Bet, Betty, Betsy, Bessie, Bess; Alexander (*x=cs*) to Allick and Sandie. What are we to say of Jack for John? It seems to be from Jacques, which is the French for our James? How came the confusion? I do not remember to have met with the name James in early English history; and it seems to have reached us from Scotland. Perhaps, as Jean and Jaques were among the commonest French names, John came into use as a baptismal name, and Jaques or Jack entered by its side as a familiar term. But this is a mere guess; and I solicit further information. John answers to the German Johann or Jehann, the Sclavonic Ivan, the Italian Giovanni (all these languages using a strengthening consonant to begin the second syllable): the French Jean, the Spanish Juan, James to the German Jacob, the Italian Giacomo, the French Jacques, the Spanish Jago. It is observable that of these, James and Giacomo alone have the *m.* Is James derived from Giacomo? How came the name into Scotland?

Of German pet-names some are formed by abbreviation; some also add *s*, as Fritz for Frieds from Friedrich, Hanns for Hann from Johann. (To this answers our *s* or *c* in the forms Betsy, Nancy, Elsie, &c.) Some take *chen* (our *kin*, as *mannikin*) as Franschen, Hannchen. Thus Catskin in the nursery ballad which appears in Mr. Halliwell's Collection, is a corruption of

Kätchen Kitty. Most of our softened words are due to the smooth-tongued Normans. The harsh Saxon Schrobbesbyrigschire, or Shropshire, was by them softened into le Comté de Salop, and both names are still used.

BENJ. H. KENNEDY.

Shrewsbury, Feb. 2. 1850.

LACEDÆMONIAN BLACK BROTH

If your readers are not already as much disgusted with Spartan Black Broth as Dionysius was with the first mouthful, I beg leave to submit a few supplementary words to the copious indications of your correspondents "R.O." and "W."

Selden says:—

> "It was an excellent question of Lady Cotton, when Sir Robert Cotton was magnifying of a shoe, which was Moses's or Noah's, and wondering at the strange shape and fashion of it: 'But, Mr. Cotton,' says she, '*are you sure it is a shoe?*'"

Now, from the following passage in Manso's *Sparta*, it would seem that a similar question might be put on the present occasion: *Are you sure that it was broth?* Speaking of the *pheiditia*, Manso says:—

> "Each person at table had as much barley-bread as he could eat; swine's-flesh, or some other meat, to eat with it, with which the famous black-sauce[2] (whose composition, without any loss to culinary art, is evidently a mystery for us) was given round, and to close the meal, olives, figs, and cheese."

In a note he continues:—

> "Some imagined that the receipt of its composition was to be found in Plutarch (*De Tuendâ Sanitate*, t. vi. p. 487.), but apparently it was only imagination. That ζωμος signified not broth, as it has been usually translated, but *sauce*, is apparent from the connection in which Athenæus used the word. To judge from Hesychius, it appears to have borne the name βαφα among the Spartans. How little it pleased the Sicilian Dionysius is well known from Plutarch (*Inst. Lacon.* t. v. 880.) and from others."

Sir Walter Trevelyan's question is soon answered, for I presume the celebrity of Spartan Black Broth is chiefly owing to the anecdote of Dionysius related by Plutarch, in his very popular and amusing *Laconic Apophthegms*, which Stobæus and Cicero evidently followed; this, and what is to be gathered from Athenæus and Julius Pollux, with a few words in Hesychius and the *Etymologicon Magnum*, is the whole amount of our information. Writers since the revival of letters have mostly copied each other, from Coelius Rhodiginus down to Gesner, who derives his conjecture from Turnebus, whose notion is derived from Julius Pollux,—and so we move in a circle. We sadly want a Greek Apicius, and then we might resolve the knotty question. I fear we must give up the notion of cuttle-fish stewed in their own ink, though some former travellers have not spoken so favourable of this Greek dish. Apicius, *De Arte Coquinariâ*, among his fish-sauces has three Alexandrian receipts, one of which will give some notion of the incongruous materials admissible in the Greek kitchen of later times:—

> "JUS ALEXANDRINUM IN PISCE ASSO.
>
> "Piper, cepam siccam, ligusticum, cuminum, orignum, apii semen, pruna damascena enucleata; passum, liquamen, defrutum, oleum, et coques."

This question Vexata it seems had not escaped the notice of German antiquaries. In Boettiger's *Kleine Shriften*, vol. iii., Sillig has printed for the first time a Dissertation, in answer to a question which might have graced your pages: "Wherewith did the Ancients spoon" [their food]? Which opens thus:—

> "Though about the composition and preparation of Spartan Black Sauce we may have only so many doubts, yet still it remains certain that it was a *jus*—boiled flesh prepared with pig's blood, salt, and vinegar, a *brodo*; and, when it was to a certain degree thickened by boiling, though not like a *Polenta* or other dough-like mass (*maza offa*), eaten with the fingers. Here, then, arises a gastronomic question, of importance in archæology; what table furniture or implements did the Spartans make use of to carry this sauce to their months? A spoon, or some substitute for a spoon, must have been at hand in order to be able to enjoy this Schwarzsauer."

It is certain at least that spoons and forks were unknown to the Spartans, and some have conjectured that a shell, and even an egg-shell, may have served the purpose. Those who are desirous of knowing more about the Table-Supellectile of the ancients, may consult Casaubon's *Notes on Athenæus*, iv. 13. p. 241.; "Barufaldo de Armis Convivialibus," in Sallengre's *Thesaurus*, iii. 741.: or Boettiger's *Dissertation* above referred to. How little ground the passage in Plutarch, *De Sanitate Tuendâ*, afforded for the composition will appear from the passage, which I subjoin, having found some difficulty in referring to it:

Οι Λακωνες υξος και 'αλας δοντες τω μαγειρω, τα λοιπα κελευουσω εν τω ιερειω ζητειν.

This only expresses the simplicity of Spartan cookery in general.

To revert to the original question propounded, however, I think we must come to the conclusion that *coffee* formed no part of the μελας ζωμος.

S.W.S.

Footnote 2: (return) Manso's word is *Tunke.*

A HINT TO INTENDING EDITORS

Allow me to suggest, as an addition to the sphere of usefulness of the "NOTES AND QUERIES," that persons preparing new editions of old writers should give an early intimation of the work on which they are engaged to the public, through your paper. Very many miscellaneous readers are in the habit of making notes in the margins of their books, without any intention of using them themselves for publication, and would be glad to give the benefit of them to any body to whom they would be welcome; but as matters are now arranged, one has no opportunity of hearing of an intended new edition until it is advertised as being in the press, when it is probably too late to send notes or suggestions; and one is also deterred from communicating with the editor from doubts whether he will not think it an intrusion: doubts which any editor who *did* wish for communications might dispel by making such an announcement as I have suggested.

R.R.

Lincoln's Inn.

NOTES UPON CUNNINGHAM'S HAND-BOOK OF LONDON

St. Giles's Pound.—The exact site of this Pound, which occupied a space of thirty feet, was the broad space where St. Giles's High Street, Tottenham Court Road, and Oxford Street meet. The vicinity of this spot was proverbial for its profligacy; thus in an old song:—

"At Newgate steps Jack Chance was found,

And bred up near *St. Giles's Pound.*"

Dudley Court, St. Giles's.—This spot was once the residence of Alice Duchess of Dudley, in the reign of Charles the Second; and afterwards of the celebrated Lord Wharton. The mansion and gardens were of considerable extent.

St. Giles's Hospital.—The celebrated Dr. Andrew Boorde rented for many years the Master's house. He is mentioned as its occupant in the deed of transfer between Lord Lisle to Sir Wymonde Carewe, dated in the last year of Henry the Eighth's reign.

Gray's Inn Lane.—Anciently called *Portpoole.* See the commission granted to the Master of the Hospital of St. Giles's, &c. to levy tolls upon all cattle, merchandize, &c., dated 1346, in Rymer's *Foedera.*

Great Queen Street, Lincoln's Inn.—Lord Herbert of Cherbury was one of the first inhabitants of this street, residing at the south side, near the east corner of Wild (or more properly *Weld*) Street, where he died in 1648. The house is still standing, and is one of fifteen built in the third year of James the First. *Powlet* and *Conway* houses, also still standing, are among the said number. The celebrated Dr. Mead (D. 1754) resided in this street.

Turnstile Lane, Holborn.—Richard Pendrell, the preserver of Charles the Second, resided here in 1668. It is supposed that Pendrell, after the Restoration, followed the king to town, and settled in the parish of St. Giles, as being near the court. Certain it is that one of Pendrell's name occurs in 1702 as overseer, which leads to the conclusion that Richard's descendants continued in the same locality for many years. A great-granddaughter of this Richard was living in 1818 in the neighbourhood of Covent Garden. Richard Pendrell died in 1674, and had a monument erected to his memory on the south-east side of the old church of St. Giles. The raising of the churchyard, subsequently, had so far buried the monument as to render it necessary to form a new one to preserve the memory of this celebrated man. The black marble slab of the old tomb at present forms the base of the new one.

EDWARD F. RIMBAULT.

Mrs. Cornelly's is stated, in vol. ii. p. 753., *to be* "the corner of Sutton Street," Soho Square, "*now D'Almaines's.*" Mrs. Cornelly's *was* at the corner of Sutton Street, but has long been pulled down: the Catholic chapel *in* Sutton Street was Mrs. Cornelly's concert, ball, and masquerade-room; and the arched entrance below the chapel, and now a wheelwright's, was the entrance for "chairs." D'Almaine's is two doors north of Sutton Street, and was built by Earl (?) Tilney, the builder of Wanstead House? The House in Soho Square has a very fine banqueting-room, the ceiling said to have been painted by Angelica Kauffmann. Tilney was fond of giving magnificent dinners, and here was always to be found "the flesh of beeves, with Turkie and other small Larks!"

Cock Lane.—The house in Cock Lane famous for its "Ghost" *is still* standing, and the back room, where "scratching Fanny" lay surrounded by princes and peers, is converted into a gas meter manufactory.

NASO.

FOLK LORE

Easter Eggs.—The custom of presenting eggs at Easter is too well known to need description; but perhaps few are aware that, like many other customs of the early Church, it had its origin in paganism.

Sir R.K. Porter (*Travels*, vol. i. p. 316.) mentions that at a period of the year corresponding to Easter, "the Feast of nooroose, or of the waters," is held, and seems to have had its origin prior to Mahometanism. It lasts for *six* days, and is supposed to be kept in commemoration of the Creation and the Deluge—events constantly synchronised and confounded in pagan cosmogonies. At this feast eggs are presented to friends, in obvious allusion to the Mundane egg, for which Ormuzd and Ahriman were to contend till the consummation of all things.

When the many identities which existed between Druidism and Magianism are considered, we can hardly doubt that this Persian commemoration of the Creation originated our Easter-eggs.

G.J.

Buns.—It has been suggested by Bryant, though, I believe, not noticed by any writer on popular customs, that the Good Friday cakes, called *Buns*, may have originated in the cakes used in idolatrous worship, and impressed with the figure of an ox, whence they were called βουν. The cow or bull was likewise, as Coleridge (*Lit. Rem.* vol. ii. p. 252.) has justly remarked, the symbol of the *Cosmos*, the prolific or generative powers of nature.

G.J.

Gloucestershire Custom.—It is a custom in Gloucestershire, and may be so in other counties, to place loose *straw* before the door of any man who beats his wife. Is this a general custom?—and if so, what is its origin and meaning?

B.

Curious Custom.—The custom spoken of by "PWCCA" (No. 11 p. 173.) was also commonly practised in one or two places in Lancashire some ten or twelve years back, but is now, I believe, obsolete. The horse was played in a similar way, but the performer was then called "Old Balls." It is no doubt a vestige of the old "hobby-horse,"—as the Norwich "Snap," who kept his place in the procession of the mayor of that good city till the days of municipal reform, was the last representative of his companion the dragon.

J.T.

[Nathan also informs us "that it is very common in the West Riding of Yorkshire, where a ram's head often takes the place of the horse's skull. Has it not an obvious connection with the 'hobby-horse' of the middle ages, and such mock pageants as the one described in Scott's *Abbot*, vol. i. chap. 14.; the whole being a remnant of the Saturnalia of the ancients?"]

QUERIES
WHITE HART INN, SCOLE

In *Songs and other Poems*, by Alex. Brome, Gent. Lond. 12mo. 1661, there is (at p. 123.) a ballad upon a sign-post set up by one Mr. Pecke, at Skoale in Norfolk. It appears from this ballad, that the sign in question had figures of Bacchus, Diana, Justice, and Prudence, "a fellow that's small, with a quadrant discerning the wind," Temperance, Fortitude, Time, Charon and Cerberus. This sign is noticed in the *Journal* of Mr. E. Browne (Sir Thomas Browne's Works, ed. Wilkin, i. 53.). Under date of 4th March, 1663-64, he says:—"About three mile further I came to Scoale, where is very handsome inne, and the noblest sighne post in England, about and upon which are carved a great many stories, as of Charon and Cerberus, of Actæon and Diana, and many other; the sighne it self is the white harte, which hangs downe carved in a stately wreath." Blomefield, in his *History of Norfolk* (8vo. edit. i. 130.), speaking of Osmundestone or Scole, has the following passage:—

> "Here are two very good inns for the entertainment of travellers; the *White Hart* is much noted in these parts, being called, by way of distinction, *Scole Inn*; the house is a large brick building, adorned with imagery and carved work in several places, as big as the life. It was built in 1655, by *John Peck*, Esq., whose arms impaling his wife's, are over the porch door. The sign is very large, beautified all over with a great number of images of large stature carved in wood, and was the work of one *Fairchild*; the arms about it are those of the chief towns and gentlemen in the county, viz. *Norwich, Yarmouth, Duke of Norfolk, Earl of Yarmouth, Bacon of Garboldisham, Hobart, Conwaleis*, impaling *Bukton, Teye, Thurston, Castleton*, and many others; *Peck's* arms are *arg.* on a chevron ingrailed, *gul.* three croslets pattee of the field; his wife's are *arg.*, a fess between two crescents in chief, a lion rampant in base *gul.*, which coat I think is borne by the name of *Jetheston.* Here was lately a very round large bed, big enough to hold fifteen or twenty couple, in imitation (I suppose) of the remarkable great bed at *Ware.* The house was in all things accommodated, at first, for large business; but the road not supporting it, it is in much decay at present; though there is a good bowling-green and a pretty large garden,

> with land sufficient for passengers' horses. The business of these two inns is much supported by the annual cock-matches that are here fought."

In Cruttwell's *Tour through the whole Island of Great Britain* (Lond. 12mo. 1801), vol. v. 208., is the following:—

> "Osmondeston, or Schole. The inn here was once remarkable for a pompous sign, with ridiculous ornaments, and is said to have cost a thousand pounds; long since decayed."

I shall be glad to be referred to any other notices of this sign, and am desirous of knowing if any drawing or engraving of it be extant.

C.H. COOPER.

Cambridge, 21st Jan. 1850.

PASSAGES FROM POPE

In addition to the query of "P.C.S.S." (No. 13. p. 201.), in which I take great interest, I would beg leave to ask what evidence there is that Quarles had a *pension?* He had, indeed, a small *place* in the household of James the First's queen, Anne; and if he had a *pension* on her death, it would have been from James, not from Charles.

I would also, in reference to Pope, beg leave to propound another query.

In the "Imitation of the 2nd Sat. Book I. of Horace," only to be found in modern editions, but attributed, I fear, too justly to Pope, there is an allusion to "poor E——s," who suffered by "*the fatal steel*," for an intrigue with a royal mistress. E——s is no doubt *John Ellis*, and the royal mistress the *Duchess of Cleveland*. (See Lord Dover's Introduction to the "Ellis Correspondence," and "Anecdotes of the Ellis Family," *Gent. Mag.* 1769. p. 328.) But I cannot discover any trace of the circumstances alluded to by Pope. Yet Ellis was a considerable man in his day;—he had been Secretary to the Lord-Lieutenant of Ireland in the reign of Charles II., and was Under-Secretary of State under William III.; he is said to have afterwards sunk into the humbler character of a "London magistrate," and to have "died in 1788, at 93 or 95, immensely rich." I should be glad of any clue to Pope's allusion.

J.W.C.

Feb 12. 1850.

"Worth makes the man, and want of it the fellow;

The rest is all but leather and prunello."

Essay on Man, Epistle IV. 203.

Will your correspondent "P.C.S.S." (No. 13), evidently a critical reader of Pope, and probably rich in the possession of various editions of his works, kindly inform me whether any commentator on the poet has traced the well-known lines that I have quoted to the "Corcillum est, quod homines facit, cætera quisquilia omnia" of Petronius Arbiter, cap. 75.? Pope had certainly both read and admired the *Satyricon*, for he says:—

"Fancy and art in gay Petronius please,

The scholar's learning with the courtier's ease."

Essay on Criticism, sect. 3

I find no note on the lines either in the edition of Warton, 9 vols. 8vo., London, 1797, or in Cary's royal 8vo., London, 1839; but the similarity strikes me as curious, and deserving further examination.

C. FORBES.

Temple.

BELVOIR CASTLE

In Nichol's *History and Antiquities of the County of Leicester*, vol. ii., part i., containing the Framland Hundred, p. 45 of the folio ed. 1795, occurs the following quotation, in reference to the rebuilding of Belvoir castle by Henry, second Earl of Rutland, in 1555:—

> "That part of the more ancient building, which was left by both unaltered, is included in the following concise description by an ingenious writer, who visited it in 1722:—
>
> 'Ædes in culmine montis sitæ, scilicet,
>
> αιπεια κολωνεν
>
> 'Εν πεδιω απανευθε περιδρομος ενθα και ενθα'
>
> aditu difficilis circa montem; cujus latera omnia horti 50 acrarum circumeunt, nisi versus Aquilonem, quò ascenditur ad ostium ædium ubi etiam antiqua jauna arcuato lapide. Versus Occidentem 8 fenestræ et 3 in sacello; et ulterior pars vetusta. Versus Aquilonem 10 fenestræ. Facies Australis et Turris de *Staunton*, in qui archiva familiæ reponuntur, extructa ante annos circa 400. Pars restat kernellata," &c. &c. &c.

The description goes on for a few more lines; but it matters not to continue them. I should be much obliged by any of your readers giving an account of who this "ingenious writer" was, and on what authority he founded the foregoing observations, as it is a subject of much interest to me and others at the present time.

ALYTHES.

Jan. 28. 1850.

MINOR QUERIES

MSS. formerly belonging to Dr. Hugh Todd.—I shall feel most grateful to any of your correspondents who can afford me any information, however imperfect, respecting the MSS. of Dr. Hugh Todd, Vicar of Penrith, and Prebendary of Carlisle, in the beginning of the last century. In the *Cat. MSS. Angliæ*, &c., 1697, is a catalogue of nineteen MSS, then in his possession, five of which are especially the subject of the present inquiry. One is a Chartulary of the Abbey of Fountains, in 4to; another is an Act Book of the Consistory Court of York, in the fifteenth century, in folio; the third is the Chapter Book of the Collegiate Church of Ripon, from 1452 to 1506; the fourth contains Extracts and Manuscripts from Records relating to the Church of Ripon; and the last is apparently a Book of the Acts of the Benefactors to that foundation. In a letter to Humphrey Lawley, dated in 1713, Dr. Todd says he was engaged in a work relating to the province of York, and the greater part of the MSS. in the catalogue above mentioned appear to have been collected as the materials.

JOHN RICHARD WALBRAN.

Falcroft, Ripon, Jan 31. 1850.

French Leave—In No. 5. I perceive several answers to the query respecting *Flemish Account*, which I presume to be the same as *Dutch Account*. Can you inform me how the very common expression *French Leave* originated?

W.G.B.

Portugal.—Can any of your geographical readers inform me if a Gazetteer of Portugal has been published within these twenty years? If there has been one, in what language, and where published? Information of the title of any good modern works on Portugal, giving an account of the minor places, would be acceptable.

NORTHMAN.

Tureen—How and whence is the term "tureen" derived?—and when was it introduced?

"At the top there was tripe in a swinging tureen."

Goldsmith's *Haunch of Venison.*

G.W.

Military Execution.—I am very anxious to be referred to the authority for the following anecdote, and remark made on it:—

> "Some officer, or state prisoner, on being led out to be shot, refused either to listen to a confessor, or to cover his eyes with a handkerchief."

The remark was, that "he refused a bandage for either mind or body." It smacks somewhat of Voltaire.

MELANION.

Change of Name.—If, as it appears by a recent decision, based, perhaps, on a former one by Lord Tenterden, that a man may alter his name as he pleases *without the royal license*, I wish to know what then, is the use of the royal license?

B.

The Symbolism of the Fir-Cone. What does the "fir-cone" in the Ninevite sculptures mean? Layard does not explain it. Is it there as the emblem of fecundity, as the pomegranate of Persia and Syria? Has it altogether the same character as the latter fruit? Then—was it carried into Hindostan *viâ* Cashmir? When? By the first wave of population which broke through the passes of the Parapamisus?

B.C.

Kentish Ballad.—When I was a boy, I can remember hearing a song sung in Kent, in praise of that country, which I never could find in print, and of which I am now glad to recollect the following stanza:—

"When Harold was invaded,

And falling lost his crown,

And Norman William waded

Through gore to pull him down;

When countries round

With fear profound,

To help their sad condition,

And lands to save,

Base homage gave,

Bold Kent made no submission."

Can any reader furnish the remainder, and state who is the author?

F.B.

Curious Monumental Brass.—I have a rubbing of a Brass, presenting some peculiarities which have hitherto puzzled me, but which probably some of your more experienced correspondents can clear up.

The Brass, from which the rubbing is taken (and which was formerly in the Abbey church of St. Albans, but when I saw it was detached and lying at the Rectory), is broken off a little below the waist; it represents an abbot, or bishop, clad in an ornamented chasuble, tunic, stole, and alb, with a maniple and pastoral staff. So far all is plain; but at the back (i.e. on the surface hidden when the Brass lay upon the floor) is engraved a dog with a collar and bells, apparently as carefully executed as any other part. Can you tell me the meaning of this? I can find no mention of the subject either in Boutell or any other authority. The fragment is about 18 inches long, and the dog about 6, more or less.

RAHERE.

Jan. 26, 1850.

Tickhill, God help me.—Can any one tell why A Tickhill man, when asked where he comes from, says, "Tickhill, God help me." Is it because the people at Tickhill are famed for misery, as the neighbouring town of Blythe seems to have been so called from its jolly citizens?

R.F. JOHNSON.

Bishop Blaize.—I should be much obliged by any reference to information respecting Bishop Blaize, the Santo Biagio of Agrigentum, and patron saint of Ragusa. Butler says little but that he was bishop of Sebaste, in Armenia, the proximity of which place to Colchis appears to me suspicious. Wonderful and horrible tales are told of him; but I suspect his patronage of wool-combers is founded on much more ancient legends. His establishment at Agrigentum must have been previous to Christianity. I have a vague remembrance of some mention of him in Higgins's *Anacalypsis*, but I have not now access to that work. I wish some learned person would do for other countries what Blunt has partly done for Italy and Sicily; that is, show the connection between heathen and Christian customs, &c.

F.C.B.

Vox et præterea nihil.—Whence come these oft-quoted words? Burton, in *The Anatomy of Melancholy* (not having the book by me, I am unable to give a reference), quotes them as addressed by some one to the nightingale. Wordsworth addresses the cuckoo similarly, vol. ii. p. 81.:—

"O, cuckoo! shall I call thee bird,

Or but a wandering voice?"

C.W.G.

Cromwell Relics.—In Noble's *Memorials of the Protectorate House of Cromwell* it is stated, in the Proofs and Illustrations, Letter N, that in 1784, there were dispersed in St. Ives a great number of swords, bearing the initials of the Protector upon them; and, further, that a large barn, which Oliver built there, was still standing, and went by the name of Cromwell's Barn; and that the farmer then renting the farm occupied by the Protector circa 1630-36, marked his sheep with the identical marking-irons which Oliver used, and which had O.C. upon them.

Can any of your correspondents inform me if any of these relics are still in existence, and, if so, where?

A.D.M.

Lines on "Woman's Will."—Many of your readers will have heard quoted the following stanza, or something like it:—

"The man's a fool who strives by force or skill

To stem the torrent of a woman's will;

For if she will, she will you may depend on't,

And if she won't, she won't, and there's an end on't."

I have heard these lines confidently attributed to Shakspeare, Byron, &c. by persons unable to verify the quotation, when challenged so to do. I can point out where the first two lines may be found with some variation. In *The Adventures of Five Hours*, a comedy translated from the Spanish of Calderon, by Samuel Tuke, and printed in the 12th volume of Dodsley's *Old Plays* (edit. 1827), in the 5th act (p. 113.), the lines run thus:—

"He is a fool, who thinks by force or skill

To turn the current of a woman's will."

I should be glad if any one could inform me by whom the latter lines were added, and where they may be found in print.

C.W.G.

Pity is akin to Love.—Where are the following words to be met with?—

"For Pity is akin to Love."

I have found very similar expressions, but never the exact words as above.

H.

REPLIES
AELFRIC'S COLLOQUY, AND THE A.-S. WORD ÆGYPE IN THE A.-S. PSALTER

In reference to MR. THORPE'S note (No. 15. p. 232.), I beg leave, with all possible respect and deference, to suggest that his joke is not quite *ad rem.*—What would do for a *beefsteak* does not help his *mistake*; for it is quite evident that *sprote* applies to fish-*swimming* and not to fish-*catching*; and I presume that "useful and sagacious" auxiliary, Dr. Kitchener himself, would hardly have ventured to deny that *fish* may *swim quickly*?

Now let us try how MR. THORPE'S proposed *salice=wicker*, or *sallow*, with or without the *basket*, will suit the context. The fisherman is asked, "Quales pisces capias? = What fish do you take?" The answer is Anguillos &c. &c. et qualescunque in amne natant salu = Eels &c. &c., and every sort whatever that in water swimmeth [wicker/sallow] basket! Let it be remembered that the question here is not, "*How* dost thou take fish?" which had been put and *answered before*, but "*What* fish dost thou take?" and then let common sense decide; for the fisherman having already mentioned that he cast *nets* and *hooks*, and [*spyrian*/spartas], i.e. *baskets*, now only replies as to the *fish* he takes.

MR. THORPE calls the A.-S. dialogue a *Gloss*; is it not rather an *interlineary version*? like those in use, in later times, of Corderius, and used for the same purpose.

I have no doubt that upon more mature consideration MR. THORPE will see that it could not be a substantive that was intended; and, as he admits my conjecture to be *specious*, that he will, in the course of his very useful labours, ultimately find it not only specious but correct. Meanwhile, I submit to his consideration, that beside the analogy of the Gothic *sprauto*, we have in Icelandic *spretta*, imperf. *spratt*, "subito movere, repente salire, emicare;" and *sprettr*, "cursus citatus," and I do think these analogies warrant my conclusion.

I embrace this opportunity of submitting another *conjecture* respecting a word in MR. THORPE'S edition of the *Anglo-Saxon Paraphrase of the Psalms.* It occurs in Ps. cvi. ver. 10., "Quid exacerbaverunt eloquium Domini," &c.,

which is rendered: "Forthon hidydan Drihtnes spræce ægwaes *ægype*." In a note MR. THORPE says: "*ægype*, non intelligo," and gives a reason for deeming the passage corrupt. To me it seems to express the generally accepted sense of *exacerbaverunt*: and here a cognate language will show us the way. Icelandic *geip*, futilis exaggeratio; *atgeipa*, exaggerare, effutire: *ægype*, then, means to *mock*, to *deride*, and is allied to *gabban*, to gibe, to jape. In the Psalter published by Spelman it is rendered: hi *gremedon* spræce godes. In Notker it is *widersprachen*, and in the two old Teutonic interlinear version of the Psalms, published by Graff, *verbitterten* and *gebittert*. Let us hear our own interesting old satirist, Piers Plouhman [Whitaker's ed. p. 365.]:

And God wol nat be gyled, quoth Gobelyn, ne be *japed*.

But I cease, lest your readers should exclaim, Res non verba. When I have more leisure for *word-catching*, should you have space, I may furnish a few more.

S.W. SINGER.

Feb. 11. 1850.

Ælfric's Colloquy.—I have my doubts whether MR. SINGER'S ingenious suggestions for explaining the mysterious word *sprote* can be sustained. The Latin sentence appears clearly to end with the word *natant*, as is not only the case in the St. John's MS., mentioned in MR. THORPE'S note, but in fact, also in the Cottonian MS. There is a point after *natant*, and then follows the word *Saliu* (not *salu*) with a capital *S*. Any person who examines the handwriting of this MS. will see that the word, whatever the transcriber may have understood by it, was intended by him to stand alone. He must, however, have written it without knowing what it meant; and then comes the difficulty of explaining how it got into the MS. from which he copied. It has always appeared to me probable that the name of some fish, having been first interlined, was afterwards inserted at random in the text, and mis-spelt by a transcriber who did not know its meaning. A word of common occurrence he would have been less likely to mistake. Can *saliu* be a mistake for *salar*, and *sprote* the Anglo-Saxon form of the corresponding modern word *sprod*, i.e. the salmon of the second year? The *salar* is mentioned by Ausonius in describing the river Moselle and its products (*Idyll.* 10, l. 128.).

"Teque inter species geminas neutrumque et utrumque,

Qui necdum salmo, nec jam salar, ambiguusque

Amborum medio fario intercepte sub ævo."

I throw out this conjecture to take its chance of refutation or acceptance. Valeat quantum!

C.W.G.

ANTONY ALSOP

"R.H." (No. 14, p. 215.) will find all, I believe, that is known respecting Antony Alsop, in that rich storehouse of materials for the literary history of the last century, Nichols's *Anecdotes*, or in Chalmers (*Biog. Dict.*), who has merely transcribed from it. The volume of *Latin Odes* your correspondent mentions, was published by Sir Francis Bernard, and printed by Bowyer. Some notice of Sir Francis Bernard will also be found in Nichols.

The *Odes* were long circulated in MS.; and I have a copy that once belonged to Thomas Warton, which seems to have been written by G. Crochly, of Christchurch College, in 1736. It contains, however, nothing that is not to be found in the printed volume. The Dedication to the Duke of Newcastle was written by Bernard, who had intended to have given a preface and copious notes, as appears by the prospectus he published: but, to our great regret, he was dissuaded from his purpose.

Alsop was a favourite with that worthy man and elegant scholar Dean Aldrich, at whose instance he published his pleasing little volume, *Fabularum Æsopicarum Delectus*, Oxon. 1698. In the preface Bentley is thus designated—"Richardum quendam Bentleium Virum in volvendis Lexicus satis diligentem:" and there is a severe attack upon him in one of the fables, which was not forgotten by the great scholar, who affects to speak of Tony Alsop the fabulist with great contempt.

I have never seen the volume of *Latin and English Poems* published in 1738; but, notwithstanding the designation, "a gentleman of Trinity College," it may be at least partly by Alsop, though he undoubtedly was of Christchurch. There are English poems by him, published both in Dodsley's and Pearch's collection, and several in the early volumes of the *Gentleman's Magazine*. I have the authority of a competent judge for saying, that the very witty, but not quite decent verses in that miscellany, vol. v. p. 216—"Ad Hypodidasculum quendam plagosum, alterum orbilium, ut uxorem duceret, Epistola hortativa." Subscribed "Kent, Lady-day, 1835"—are Alsop's. He took the degree of M.A. in 1696, and of B.D. in 1706, and, by favour of the Bishop of Winchester, got a prebend in his cathedral, and the rectory of Brightwell, Berks. He was accidentally drowned in a ditch leading to his garden gate, in 1726. There is good reason to believe that a MS. life of him is to be found among the Rawlinson MSS., which it may be worth while to consult.

It will be remembered that Christchurch was the head-quarters of the phalanx of wits opposed to Bentley.

"Nor wert thou, Isis, wanting to the day,

[Tho' Christchurch long kept prudishly away,"]

is Pope's ironical banter; and he has not failed to mention Alsop and Freind in Bentley's speech:—

"Let Freind affect to speak as Terence spoke,

And Alsop never but like Horace joke,"

where the note says, "Dr. Antony Alsop, a happy imitator of the Horatian style."

Indeed, Alsop seems to have been duly esteemed and appreciated by his contemporaries; and every tasteful scholar will concur in the opinion that his truly elegant Sapphics deserve a place among the few volumes of modern Latin verse, which he would place near Cowper's more extensively known favourite, Vinny Bourne.

S.W.S.

Antony Alsop, respecting whom a query appears in No. 14. p. 215., was of Christchurch, under the famous Dr. Aldrich, by whom the practice of smoking was so much enjoyed and encouraged. The celebrated Sapphic ode, addressed by Alsop to Sir John Dolben, professes to have been written with a pipe in his mouth:—

"Dum tubum, ut mos est meus, ore versans,

Martiis pensans quid agam calendas,

Pone stat Sappho monitisque miscet

Blanda severis."

Ant. Alsop took his degree of M.A. March 23. 1696, B.D. Dec. 1706. He died June 10, 1726; and the following notice of his death appears in the *Historical Register* for that year:—

"Dy'd Mr. Antony Alsop, Prebendary of Winchester, and Rector of Brightwell, in the county of Berks. He was killed by falling into a ditch that led to his garden door, the path being narrow, and part of it foundering under his feet."

I believe Alsop was not the author of a volume by a gentleman of Trinity College, and that he never was a member of that society; but that doubt is easily removed by reference to the entry of his matriculation at Oxford.

W.H.C.

Temple.

"R.H." inquires, whether Antony Alsop was at Trinity College before he became a student of Christchurch? I have considered it to be my duty to examine the Admission Registers of Trinity College in my possession since the foundation of the college; and I can only say, that I do not find the name in any of them. That he was at Christchurch, and admitted there as a student, is recorded by his biographers. It is also said, that he was elected at once from Westminster to Christchurch, where he took the degree of M.A. March 23. 1696, and that of B.D. Dec. 12. 1706. He was soon distinguished by Dean Aldrich as worthy of his patronage and encouragement. He was consequently appointed tutor and censor, and in course of time left college, on his promotion to a prebendal stall in Winchesser Cathedral by Sir Jonathan Trelawney, the then Bishop, with the rectory of Brightwell, near Wallingford; at which latter place he chiefly resided till the time of his death, which happened by an accident, June 10. 1726. Sir Francis Bernard, Bart., who had himself been a student of Christchurch, published the 4to. volume of *Latin Odes* mentioned by "R.H.," Lond. 1753; for which he had issued *Proposals*, &c., so early as July, 1748. In addition to these *Odes*, four English poems by Alsop are said to be in Dodsley's collection, one in Pearch's, several in the early volumes of the *Gentleman's Magazine*, and some in *The Student*. Dr. Bentley calls him, rather familiarly, "Tony Alsop, editor of the *Æsopian Fables*;" a work published by him at Oxford, in 1698, 8 vo., in the preface to which he took part against Dr. Bentley, in the dispute with Mr. Boyle.

J.I.

Trinity College, Oxford.

REPLIES TO MINOR QUERIES

Origin of the Word "Snob".—I think that *Snob* is not an archaism, and that it cannot be found in any book printed fifty years ago. I am aware that in the north of England shoe-makers are still sometimes called *Snobs*; but the word is not in Brockett's *Glossary of North Country Words*, which is against its being a genuine bit of northern dialect.

I fancy that *Snobs* and *Nobs*, as used in vulgar parlance, are of classic derivation; and, most probably, originated at one of the Universities, where they still flourish. If a *Nob* be one who is *nobilis*, a *Snob* must be one who is *s[ine] nob[ilitate]*. Not that I mean to say that the *s* is literally a contraction of *sine*; but that, as in the word slang, the *s*, which is there prefixed to *language*, at once destroys the better word, and degrades its meaning; and as, in Italian, an *s* prefixed to a primitive word has a privative effect—e.g. *calzare*, "to put on shoes and stockings;" *scalzare*, "to put them off:" *fornito*, "furnished;" *sfornito*, "unfurnished," &c.; as also the *dis*, in Latin (from which, possibly, the aforesaid *s* is derived), has the like reversing power, as shown in *continue* and *discontinue*—so *nob*, which is an abbreviation of *nobilis*, at once receives the most ignoble signification on having an *s* put before it.

The word *Scamp*, meaning literally a fugitive from the field, one *qui ex campo exit*, affords another example of the power of the initial *s* to reverse the signification of a word.

All this, Mr. Editor, is only conjecture, in reply to "ALPHA's" query (No. 12 p. 185.); but perhaps you will receive it, if no better etymology of the word be offered.

A.G.

Ecclesfield, Jan. 21. 1850.

Derivation(?) of "Snob" and "Cad."—I am informed by my son, who goeth to a Latin school, that *Snob* (which is a word he often useth) cometh of two Latin words; to wit, "*sine obolo*"—as who should say, "one that hath not a cross to bless himself." He saith, that the man behind the omnibus is called "*Cad*," "*a non cadendo*." Your humble servant,

THE GOVERNOR.

Mr. Macaulay and Bishop Burnet.—The passage in which Mr. Macaulay calls Burnet "a rash and partial writer," alluded to by your correspondent in No.

3. p. 40., occurs towards the end of his Essay on "Sir William Temple," p. 456. of the new edition in one volume.

ETONIENSIS.

Circulation of the Blood.—"A.W." (No. 13. p. 202.) is referred to Smith's *Dictionary of Biography*, article NEMESIUS.

J.E.B. MAYOR.

Genealogy of European Sovereigns.—I send the full title of a book which I would recommend to your correspondent "Q.X.Z.," (No. 6. p. 92.):—

> GÉNÉALOGIE ASCENDANTE,
>
> JUSQU'AU QUATRIÈME DÉGRÉ INCLUSIVEMENTS,
>
> De tous les Rois et Princes de Maisons souveraines de l'Europe actuellement vivans; réduite en CXIV. Tables de XVI. Quartiers, composées selon les Principes du Blazon; avec une Table Générale.
>
> ---
>
> "La noblesse, Daugaux, n'est point une chimère, Quand sous l'étroite loi d'une vertu sévère, Un homme, issu d'un sang fécond en demi-dieux, Suit, comme toi, la trace où marchaient ses ayeux." Boileau, S.v.
>
> ---
>
> A BERLIN:
>
> Au Dépens de l'Autheur: se vend chez Etienne de Bourdeaux, Libraire; imprimé chez Frédéric Guillaume Birnstiel.
>
> MDCCLXVIII.

I presume that it is of some rarity, never having met with any other copy than the one from which I transcribed this title.

Some of your correspondents may, perhaps, be able to give the name of the Author who, as far as I have had occasion to refer, seems to have done his work carefully.

T.W.

Sir Stephen Fox.—I have seen it stated in some biographical dictionary, that Sir Stephen Fox was a younger brother of "John Fox, Esq.," who was a devoted Royalist at the time of the great Rebellion, and fought at the battle of Worcester, and after the Restoration was Clerk of the Acatry, in the household of Charles the Second.

Mr. Suckling, in his *History of Suffolk*, claims for a family some time seated at Stradbrook, in that county, a consanguinity with the descendants of Sir Stephen.

On an altar-tomb in Stadbrook churchyard are inscribed notices of many members of this family, but without dates. One is rather extraordinary, making the lives of a father and son together to amount to 194 years. Amongst them is this:—

> "Here is hourly expected, Simon the next descendant, with his son Simon, who died young, tho' still preserved to be interr'd with his father at the earnest request of his pious mother the Lady Hart. And also Major John Fox, with his issue, who during the late rebellion loyally behav'd himself, undergoing with great courage not only the danger of the field, but many severe imprisonments."

The arms on this tomb differ from those of Lords Ilchester and Holland, being simply three foxes' heads erased.

Should this note supply a clue for your correspondent "VULPES" to identify Major John Fox with the brother of Sir Stephen, on knowing that he has found the scent I shall be able to assist him in unearthing the whole litter.

VENATOR.

French Maxim.—The maxim inquired after by "R.V." (No. 14. p. 215.) undoubtedly belongs to Rochefoucault. I have met with a somewhat similar passage in Massillon:—

> "Le vice rend hommage à la vertu en s'honorant de sus apparences."

J.B.M.

Feb. 5. 1850.

Shipster.—A *scip-steora* among our Anglo-Saxon ancestors was a pilot ("*ship-steerer*"). The word has descended to our own times in the surname of the family Shipster. As a common noun it was not obsolete in the days of Wynkyn de Worde, who printed that curious production "*Cock Lorelle's Bote*," one line of which runs thus:—

"With gogle-eyed Tomson, *shepster* of Lyn."

It is pretty certain, however, that this masculine occupation was not the one followed by "Marie Fraunceys de Suthwerk!"

Pray accept this "Reply" for what it is worth. Perhaps I might have done better by meeting Mr. John R. Fox's "Query" (No. 14. p. 216.) with another. Should not the designation of Marie F. be *Spinster* instead of Shipster?

MARK ANTONY LOWER.

Lewes, Feb. 2.

Sparse.—Permit me to refer your correspondent "C. FORBES" for a reply to his query, p. 215. of your last Number, to the article "Americanism" in the *Penny Cyclopædia*, the author of which observes:—

> "*Sparse* is, for any thing we know, a new word, and well applied; the Americans say a *sparse* instead of a scattered population; and we think the term has a more precise meaning than scattered, and is the proper correlative of *dense*."

In the *Imperial Dictionary* (avowedly based upon Webster's American work, which I cannot at this moment refer to in its original form), the word in question is given both as an adjective and as a verb, and the derivatives "sparsed," "sparsedly," "sparsely," and "sparseness," are also admitted. The reference given for the origin of "sparse" is to the Latin "*sparsus*, scattered, from *spargo*;" and the definitions are, 1. "Thinly scattered, set or planted here and there; as, a *sparse* population:" and, 2., as a botanical term, "not opposite, not alternate, nor in any regular order; applied to branches, leaves, peduncles, &c."

J.T. STANESBY.

Cosmopolis—Complutensian Polyglot.—Though in considerable haste, I must send replies to the fourth and eighth queries of my friend Mr. Jebb, No. 14. p. 213.

Cosmopolis was certainly Amsterdam. That the *Interpretationes paradoxæ quatuor Evangeliorum*, by Christophorus Christophori Sandius, were there printed, appears from this writer's *Bibliotheca Anti-Trinitarionum*, p. 169., Freistad, 1684. I may add that "Coloniæ" signifies "Amstelædami" in the title-page of

Sandius's *Nucleus Historiæ Ecclesiasticæ*, 1676, and in the *Appendix Addendorum*, 1678, 4to.

With regard to the MSS. used in the formation of the text of the *Complutensian Polyglot*, Mr. Jebb will find an account of their discovery in a letter addressed by Dr. James Thompson to the editor of *The Biblical Review*. See also *The Irish Ecclesiastical Journal* for April 1847.

R.G.

Complutensian Polyglot.—The following extract from "The Prospectus of a Critical Edition of the New Testament," by the learned Mr. S. Prideaux Tregelles, affords a satisfactory reply to Mr. Jebb's query, No. 14. p. 212.:—

> "However there is now more certainty as to the MSS. belonging to the University of Alcala. Dr. James Thompson has published (*Biblical Review*, March, 1847), the result of inquiries made thirty years ago by Dr. Bowring, and more recently by himself. Hence it appears that all the MSS. which formerly were known as belonging to Cardinal Ximenes, and which were preserved in the library of Alcala, are now with the rest of that library, at Madrid....Dr. José Gutierrez, the present librarian at Madrid, communicated to Dr. J. Thomson a catalogue of the Complutensian MSS., and from this it appears that the principal MSS. used in the Polyglott are all safely preserved."

J. MILNER BARRY.

Totnes, Feb. 6. 1850.

Christmas Hymn.—Your correspondent "E.V." (No. 13. p. 201.) asks for the author of the Christmas Hymn—

"Hark! the Herald Angels sing."

I believe it to be the composition of the Rev. Charles Wesley, the younger brother of the celebrated John Wesley: he was born in 1708, and died in 1788. He was the author of many of the hymns in his brother's collection, which are distinguished for their elegance and simplicity. I am not able to find out, for certain, whether he had another name; if he had, it was probably the occasion of the initials (J.C.W.) your correspondent mentions.

J.K.R.W.

Sir Jeffery Wyattville.—Sir Jeffery Wyattville, respecting whom "J.P." inquires (No. 14. p. 215.), was knighted at Windsor Castle, Dec. 9, 1828., on the king entering into possession after the restoration.

S.G.

> [To which may be added, on the information of our valued correspondent "C.," "that it was about 1824 that Mr. Wyatt, being appointed by George IV. to conduct the improvements at Windsor Castle, had the absurd ambition of distinguishing himself from the other architects of his name by changing it to *Wyattville.* This produced the following epigram in, I think, the *Morning Chronicle*:—

"'Let GEORGE whose restlessness leaves nothing quiet,

Change, if he will, the good old name of *Wyatt*;

But let us hope that their united skill

May not make *Windsor Castle—Wyattsville!*'"]

"Peruse."—In reply to the question of "H.W." (No. 14. p. 215.), although from want of minute reference I have been unable to find, in the original edition, the quotation from Frith's works, I beg leave to suggest that the word "Peruse" is a misprint, and that the true reading is "Pervise." To this day the first examination at Oxford, commonly called the "Little-Go," is "Responsiones in *Parviso.*" It must not, however, be supposed that "Pervise," or "Parvise," is derived from the Latin "Parvus;" the origin, according to Spelman and succeeding etymologists, is the French "Le Parvis," a church porch.

In London the Parvis was frequented by serjeants at law: see Chaucer, *Prol. Cant. Tales.* There is a difference of opinion where it was situated: see Tyrwhitt's *Gloss.* The student in ecclesiastical history may compare *Leo Allatius de Templis Græcorum*, p. 44.

T.J.

Autograph Mottoes of Richard Duke of Gloucester and Harry Duke of Buckingham. (No. 9. p. 138.)—There can be no doubt that "Mr. NICOLS" is somewhat wrong in his interpretation of the Duke of Buckingham's Motto. It is evident that both mottoes are to be read continuously, and that "souene" is the third person singular of a verb having "loyaulte" for its nominative case. It appears to me that the true reading of the word is "soutienne," and that the meaning of the motto is "My feelings of loyalty often sustain me in my duty to the King when I am tempted to join those who bear no good feeling towards him." So that we shall have in English,

Loyalty binds me }

Richard Gloucester. }

Often sustains me }

Harry Buckingham. }

ARUN.

Boduc.—Your correspondent "P." (No. 12, p. 185.) seems to consider the "prevailing opinion," that *Boduc* or *Boduoc* on the British coin must be intended for our magnanimous Queen Boadicea, to be merely a "pleasing vision," over which he is "*sorry* to cast a cloud." Yet his own remark, that the name Budic (a mere difference in spelling) is often found among families of the Welsh in Brittany, and that the name was once common in England, serves only to confirm the common opinion that *Boduoc* on the coins was intended as the name of the British Queen.

Dio expressly writes her name in Greek Boudouica, which approaches nearly to Budic. In Cornwall we still find Budock, the name of a parish and of a saint. In Oxford there was a church formerly called from St. Budoc, long since destroyed. Leland mentions a Mr. Budok, and his manor place, and S. Budok Church. His opinion was, that "this Budocus was an Irisch man, and cam into Cornewalle, and ther dwellid." Whether there was a Regulus of Britain of this name, is not material. I am not prepared to cast a cloud over it, if it should be found. Our motto should be, "ex fumo dare lucem," &c.

ANTINEPHELEGERETA.

Oxford.

Annus Trabeationis.—I am sure that you will allow me to correct an oversight in your reply to a query of "G.P.," in No. 7. p. 105. You have attributed to Du Cange a sentence in the Benedictine addition to his explanation of the term *Trabeatio.* (*Glossar.* tom. vi. col. 1158. Venet. 1740.) This word certainly signifies the Incarnation of Christ, an not his Crucifixion. Besides the occurrence of "trabea carnis indutus," at the commencement of a sermon on S. Stephen by S. Fulgentius Ruspensis, I have just now met with the expressions, "trabea carnis velatus," and "carnis trabea amicti," in a copy of the *editio princeps* of the Latin version of Damascen's books in defence of Image-worship, by Godefridus Tilmannus, fol. 30 b. 39 a, 4to. Paris, 1555.

R.G.

MISCELLANIES

Pursuits of Literature.—The lines upon the pursuits of literature, quoted by you at p. 212., remind me of some others, which I have heard ascribed to Mr. Grattan, and are as follows:—

"'Tis well, Pursuits of Literature!

But who, and what is the pursuer,

A Jesuit cursing Popery:

A railer preaching charity;

A reptile, nameless and unknown,

Sprung from the slime of Warburton,

Whose mingled learning, pride, and blundering,

Make wise men stare, and set fools wondering."

X.

Doctor Dobbs and his Horse Nobbs.—I remember having read somewhere of "Doctor Dobbs and his horse Nobbs," but where I cannot now recall. I only remember one anecdote. The horse Nobbs was left, one cold night, outside a cottage, whilst the Doctor was within officiating as accoucheur (I believe); when he was ready to start, and came out, he found the horse apparently dead. The Doctor was miles from home, and, as the horse was dead, and the night dark, in place of walking home, he, with his host, dragged the horse into the kitchen, and skinned him, by way of passing the time profitably. But, lo! when the skinning was finished, the horse gave signs of returning animation. What was to be done? Doctor Dobbs, fertile in resources, got sheepskins and sewed them on Nobbs, and completely clothed him therein; and—mirabile dictu!—the skins became attached to the flesh, Nobbs recovered, and from thenceforward carried a *woolly* coat, duly shorn every summer, to the profit of Doctor Dobbs, and to the wonder and admiration of the neighbourhood.

I have also read somewhere that Coleridge told the story of "Doctor Dobbs and his horse Nobbs" to Southey at Oxford.

J.M.B.

Dr. Dobbs and his Horse Nobbs.—Although of small moment, it is, perhaps, worth recording, that a Doctor Daniel Dove, of Doncaster, and his horse

Nobbs, form the subjects of a paper in "The Nonpareil, or the Quintessence of Wit and Humour," published in 1757, and which, there can be little doubt, was the source whence Southey adopted, *without alteration*, the names so well known to all readers of the *Doctor*.

JNO. SUDLOW.

Manchester.

Seeing the communication of "P.C.S.S." (p. 73.), reminds me of a note taken from our Parish Register:—

"1723. Feb. 10. 'Dorothy Dove, gentlewoman, bur.'"

I have never seen the name in connection with Doncaster before or since the above date.

J.S.

Doncaster, Jan. 15.

——SI PROPIUS STES,

TE CAPIET MINUS.

(From the Latin of Vincent Bourne.)

Glide down the Thames by London Bridge, what time

St. Saviour's bells strike out their evening chime;

Forth leaps the ompetuous cataract of sound,

Dash'd into noise by countless echoes round.

Pass on—it follows—all the jarring notes

Blend in celestial harmony, that floats

Above, below, around: the ravish'd ear

Finds all the fault its own—it was TOO NEAR.

RUFUS.

St. Evona's Choice.—To your citation of Ben Jonson's exceptional case of the Justice Randall as "a lawyer an honest man," in justice add the name of the learned and elegant author of *Eunomus*; for Mr. Wynne himself tells the story of St. Evona's choice (Dialogue II. p. 62. 3rd ed. Dublin, 1791), giving his authority in the following note:—

> "The story here dressed up is told in substance in a small book published in 1691, called a *Description of the Netherlands*," p. 58.

In strict law, Sir, the profession may in courts of Momus be held bound by the act of the respectable but unlucky St. Evona; but in equity, let me respectfully claim release, for Evona was a *churchman*.

A TEMPLAR.

> [We gladly insert our correspondent's "claim to release," but doubt whether he can establish it; inasmuch as St. Ivo or Evona, canonized on account of his great rectitude and profound knowledge both of civil and canon law, was both lawyer and churchman, like the CLERICUS so recently discussed in our columns; and clearly sought for and obtained his patron saint in his legal character.]

Muffins and Crumpets, &c.—Not being quite satisfied with the etymology of "muffin," in p. 205., though brought by Urquhart from Phoenicia and the Pillars of Hercules, I am desirous of seeking additional illustration. Some fancy that "coffee" was known to Athenæus, and that he saw it *clearly* in the "black broth" of the Lacedæmonian youth. In the same agreeable manner we are referred to that instructive and entertaining writer for the corresponding luxury of "muffins." *Maphula*, we are told, was one of those kinds of bread named as such by Athenæus; that is to say, "a cake baked on a hearth or griddle." If we need go so far, why not fetch our muffins from Memphis, which is *Môph* in Hebrew? (See *Hosea*, ix. 6.) It is, perhaps, *mou-pain*, in old French, *soft bread*, easily converted into *mouffin*. So "crumpet" may be a corruption of *crumpâte* a paste made of fine flour, slightly baked. The only difficulty would then be in the first syllable, concerning, which the ingenuity of your various correspondents, Mr. Editor, may be exercised to some effect. Is it connected with the use of the *crimping* irons in producing these delicacies?

HYPOMAGIRUS.

Oxford.

Dulcarnon.—Dulcarnon is one of those words in Chaucer which Tyrwhitt professes that he does not understand. It occurs in *Trolius and Creseide*, book iii. 931.933. Creseide says:—

"I am, til God me better minde sende,

At *Dulcarnon*, right at my witt'is ende.

Quod Pandarus ye nece, wol ye here,

Dulcarnon clepid is fleming[3] of wretches."

This passage of *Trolius and Creseide* is quoted in the life of Sir Thomas More, given in Wordsworth's *Ecclesiastical Biography*. More's daughter said to him, when he was in prison, "Father, I can no further goe; I am come, as Chaucer said of Cressid Dulcarnon, to my witt's end."

Has this passage been satisfactorily explained since Tyrwhitt's time? The epithet "Dulcarnon" is mentioned in a note to the translation of Richard de Bury's *Philobiblon*, London, 1832. I give the note in full. It is in reference to the word "Ellefuga":—

> "This word was a pons asinorum to some good Grecians,—but that is probably its meaning[4]; at least making it the name of a problem gets over all difficulty. The allusion is to the flight of Helle, who turned giddy in taking a flying leap, mounted on a ram, and fell into the sea;—so weak a head fails in crossing the pons. The problem was invented by Pythagoras, 'and it hath been called by barbarous writers of the latter time Dulcarnon,'—*Billingsley*. This name may have been invented after our author's time. Query δολκαρηνον."

If we take the words "Dulcarnon" in this sense, it will help to explain the passage in the *Troilus and Creseide*.

E.M.B.

Bishop Barnaby.—The origin of the term "Bishop Barnaby," as applied to the Lady-bird, is still unexplained.

I wish to observe, as having some possible connexion with the subject, that the word "Barnaby" in the seventeenth century appears to have had a particular political signification.

For instance, I send you a pamphlet (which you are welcome to, if you will accept of it) called "*The Head of Nile, or the Turnings and Windings of the Factious since Sixty, in a dialogue between Whigg and Barnaby*," London, 1681. In this dialog, Whigg, as might be expected, is the exponent of all manner of abominable opinions, whilst Barnaby is represented as the supporter of orthodoxy.

Again, in the same year was published Durfey's comedy, "*Sir Barnaby Whigg*," the union of the two names indicating that the knight's opinions were entirely regulated by his interest.

Q.D.

P.S. The pamphlet above alluded to affords another instance of the use of the word "Factotum," at page 41.: "before the Pope had a great house there, and became Dominus Factotum, Dominus Deus noster Papu."

Barnacles.—In *Speculum Mundi, or a Glass representing the Face of the World*, by John Swan, M.A., 4th edit., 1670, is the following mention of the Barnacle goose (pp. 243, 244.):—

> "In the north parts of *Scotland*, and in the places adjacent, called *Orchades*, are certain trees found, whereon there groweth a certain kind of shell-fish, of a white colour, but somewhat tending to a russet; wherein are contained little living creatures. For in time of maturity the shells do open, and out of them by little and little grow those living creatures; which falling into the water when they drop out of their shells, do become fowls, such as we call *Barnacles* or *Brant Geese*; but the other that fall upon the land, perish and come to nothing."

The author then quotes the passage from Gerard where mention is made of the Barnacle.

HENRY KERSLEY.

Ancient Alms-Dishes.—I have one of these dishes; diameter 1 foot 4-3/4 inches, and its height 1-1/2 inch. The centre is plain, without any device, and separated from the circle of inscription by a bold embossed pattern.

The inscription is *Der infrid gehwart*, in raised (not engraved) capital letters, 1 inch long, repeated three times in the circle. Mine is a handsome dish of mixed metal; yielding, when struck, a fine sound like that of a gong. It has devices of leaves, &c. engraved on the broad margin, but no date.

I have seen another such dish, in the collection of the late William Hooper, Esq., of Ross, part of which (and I think the whole of the under side) had been enamelled, as part of the enamel still adhered to it. In the centre was engraved the temptation in Eden; but it was without legend or date.

P.H.F.

Why the American Aborigines are called Indians. —I have often wondered how the aborigines of America came to be called Indians; and for a considerable time I presumed it to be a popular appellation arising from their dark colour. Lately, however, I fell in with a copy of *Theatrum Orbis Terrarum.* Antwerp, 1583, by Abraham Ortelius, geographer to the king; and, in the map entitled *Typus Orbis Terrarum.* I find America called *America, sive India Nova.* How it came to get the name of *India Nova* is of course another question, and one which at present I cannot answer.

NORTHMAN.

Footnote 3: (return) Fleming; banishing? from *fleme*, A.S. to banish.

Footnote 4: (return) "Helleflight," as given in the translation, p. 178.

CPSIA information can be obtained
at www.ICGtesting.com
Printed in the USA
LVHW041021020323
740706LV00008B/1110

9 789356 898028